The Poetry of an Escapist

Harper Peters

Copyright © 2020 by Harper Peters

All rights reserved.

ISBN: 9798556469488

DEDICATION
I dedicate this book to everyone.

The Poetry of an Escapist

CAVE

I am in a dark rocky cave.
Water is pouring in fast.
I panic as I start to think about dying,
and I think about my past.

Rocks fall into the water.
A beam of light shines in my hazel eyes.
Hopeful, I climb upward.
Maybe this isn't my demise.

My hands are sore from digging.
They start to bleed.
Finally, I feel a slight breeze on my dirty face.
I crawl out of this small, cold, and lonely space.

I am free once again.
I don't take for granted this calmness
over me.
Because I know at any time I can be,
put right back into the cave of anxiety.

BOTTLE

I kept my emotions in a bottle.
They moved around very contained.
People said to let them out.
But I didn't want to feel pain.

I kept my emotions in a bottle.
They started to fight with each other inside.
They were training and getting stronger.
But denying them was how I survived.

I'd study them through the glass.
I'd watch them scream to be released.
As time passed, numbness came over me.

No one could touch me there.
I was alone, even when people surrounded me.
Feeling nothing seemed right and comfortable.
I'd cringe at the thought of being vulnerable.

Still, back and forth I'd go,
with the idea of letting my emotions free.
I had the belief revealing them,
would give people power over me.

One day, orderly words flowed into my mind.

The Poetry of an Escapist

They were all yearning to be written.
They didn't want to be confined.
I decided to write those demanding words.
Finally, granting me peace of mind.

LAUGH

I miss hearing you laugh,
at my horrible jokes.
No one else thought I was that funny.

I wish I could have,
saved your laugh,
in a conch shell.
I'd pick it up,
when I have another joke to tell.

Then hold it to my ear,
to hear your laughter.
You were a great mother.

You would listen.
You were there.
You cared.

You were perfect the way you were.
What I wouldn't give,
to hear you laughing once more.

BREAK

Sometimes my thoughts are hidden deep in
the sea.
I don't mean to be as cold as the water.
But I can be.

I descend 30 feet.
Wanting no one,
near me.

The world takes,
and takes,
and takes.

I need a break,
a break,
a break.

Sometimes my thoughts are as dark as the
black sea.
I need some silence to internalize.
I need to be free.

I swim around,
wandering.
Admiring marine life,
pondering.

Then, I ascend slowly.
Stopping to decompress,
until all the negative energy,
has left.

SWEET CHILD

Sweet child,
put yourself first.
Don't chase after boys.
They only want to quench their thirst.

Sweet child,
concentrate on yourself.
Don't try to win a boys' attention.
They don't care about what you do.

Sweet child,
you have so much to offer this world.
Focus on learning something new.
You are a confident, creative, and intelligent
girl.
The universe has something greater planned
for you.

Sweet child,
when you have traveled the earth,
figured out what you like,
found what you love,
and can stand on your own two feet,
there will be someone you will meet.
He will join you in the middle.
And, he will see,
how you make,

this world a better place.

SELF-PORTRAIT

My self-portrait,
is vividly painted in thickly layered oils.
All my parts are symmetrical and pleasing to
the eye.
So bold and commanding,
it comes to life.

I have a long white silk elegant gown.
I don't have a wrinkle in my clothes or
brown hair out of place.
My surroundings are inviting and classic.
And I have the most attractive face.

My eyes are wild and mysterious,
and my lips are luscious and sweet.
My thoughts are strong and kind,
and my intentions are never mean.

There is a tree outside my bedroom
window,
that makes my room smell of pine.
Sometimes I stand on the balcony
knowing everything will be fine.

When I look at my self-portrait,
I lift my self-confidence like a hot air
balloon,

and desire all these details to be true.

CASTLE

I'm hiding in a brick castle.
No one can break my armor.
No one can pierce my skin.
Surely the world will eat me alive,
if I let them all in.

I'm in my bedroom,
next to a stone fireplace.
Listening for unfamiliar creaks in the floorboard,
while holding my freshly sharpened sword.

Sweating from the armor and fire,
even though it is cold outside.
I think about the people that would be disappointed if
I died.

Vicious soldiers guard me.
They are all waiting for their objective.
Warriors try to fight their way in.
Some will die, and some will live.

A bloody mote surrounds my castle,
crammed with hungry sharks.
They are waiting for their next victim,
as the sky becomes dark.

A flawless exterior means nothing to me.

The Poetry of an Escapist

Time will separate,
those with pure hearts,
from those with selfish ones.
I'll have the drawbridge lowered,
for those exhibiting perseverance and beautiful souls.
Everyone else should flee,
because many heads will roll.

A worthy warrior has found me in my hiding place,
and gently reaches for my hand.
I choose him to be king,
and assist me in ruling the land.

Together we end the chaos,
and the people feel safe.
Tonight the king and queen sleep in peace,
next to a warm fireplace.

SURFING ON AN ILLUSION

My body is weak
when you speak
I fall 6 feet
crushing through concrete.
I rise from the rubble
without too many scars or scrapes
Your voice sends me on a mental **escape**.
Now, I'm surfing on sound waves
morning, noon, and night,
during high and low tide.
Drenched in your words,
I don't ever want to be dry.
I'd watch your soft lips move
to form words until the sun turns red
Billions of years wouldn't be long enough
to hear such a pure voice in my head.

THE PERFORMER

It is unfortunate how your fate
did not turn out as great
as your God-given talent
that made you sparkle
like sunlight on the ocean.

Few people are lucky to have apparent abilities,
with many people wanting them to succeed.
You were fascinating to watch, indeed.

While sitting on our couches, we watched you with
admiration, hope, and inspiration.
You convincingly spoke every sentence, every word,
and every syllable with passion.

Named after a water body at birth,
no one knew how much you would offer the world,
or how much your uniqueness would be worth.

You grew up differently, which briefly protected you
and made you wise beyond your years.
The camera captured your mastery.
Your flawless performances bring me to tears.

The Poetry of an Escapist

Dealing with my demons is much more complicated than being an escapist.

ABOUT THE AUTHOR

Harper Peters grew up in the United States on the east coast. She writes poetry in her spare time as a creative outlet.

BOOKS

A Life in Poems
The Poetry of an Escapist
My Heart is Still Beating

Share reviews of her books on Goodreads.com

Follow Harper Peters on her Amazon author page to learn about new releases.

Website: Harper-Peters.com

The Poetry of an Escapist

The Poetry of an Escapist

Made in the USA
Middletown, DE
18 June 2021